G000021952

# Wine

## A PRIMER

# Wine
## A PRIMER

**Thomas Conklin**

Ariel Books

◆

Andrews and McMeel
Kansas City

*Wine: A Primer*
copyright © 1992 by Armand Eisen.
All rights reserved. Printed in Hong Kong. No part of
this book may be used or reproduced in any manner
whatsoever without written permission except in
the case of reprints in the context of reviews.
For information write Andrews and McMeel, a
Universal Press Syndicate Company, 4900 Main
Street, Kansas City, Missouri 64112.

10 9 8 7 6 5 4 3
ISBN: 0-8362-3013-2
Library of Congress Catalog Card Number:
91-77096

Design: Tilman Reitzle and Michael Hortens

# Table of Contents

# Introduction

There is nothing like wine for conjuring up feelings of contentment and goodwill. It is less of a drink than an experience, an evocation, a spirit. It produces sensations that defy description. When one attempts it, the experience floats away, like a half-forgotten memory or the elusive scent of perfume.

The pleasure of wine comes partly from the company of good friends and the taste of good food, partly from the remembrance of things past. It is the result of thousands of years of study and experimentation, as well as the vagaries of climate and weather. This product, the happy combination of art and nature, yields a nearly infinite variety of subtle pleasures. This book will guide the first steps of the new wine lover down a long and pleasant path.

# History

## Ancient Roots

The enjoyment of wine dates back to the very beginnings of the history of mankind. Genesis tells us that when Noah stepped off the ark, his first act was to plant a vineyard and make wine. (And his second act was to drink it to excess!) There may be some historical basis to the biblical legend. The exact moment in history when humans first tasted wine is unknown, but the oldest evidence of cultivated vines — seed fossils seven thousand years old — have been found in the Caucacus Mountains, literally in the shadow of Mount Ararat.

The ancient Persians had their own

legend to describe the origins of wine. According to the legend, the Persian King Jemsheed loved grapes. He hid them in his cellar in jars marked "poison" so that he could enjoy them all year long. The grapes began to ferment within the jars. One day, a concubine, distraught over falling out of the king's favor, tried to commit suicide by drinking out of the jars. She fell into a deep sleep, and when she awoke began to tell of the wonderful dreams she had had. Thus, according to the Persians, were the magical properties of wine discovered.

Although the actual moment that wine was first made is lost to history, we do know for a fact that the Egyptians had mastered the techniques of wine making over five thousand years ago. Certain Egyptian tomb paintings depict the process in detail, and the steps shown would be easily recognized by any wine maker today.

Both the Greeks and the Romans made wine a central part of their culture. There were four festivals a year in Greece, each held around the process of making wine. One festival, dedicated to Dionysus, the god of wine, developed into the dramatic competition that gave birth to tragedy and comedy. Evenings given over to wine drinking and philosophical discussions were central to Athenian culture. Those evenings, called *symposia*, were recorded for all of history in Plato's dialogues. Wine was integral to Greek medicine, too. Hippocrates prescribed wine for maladies ranging from bee stings and snake bites to mental illness.

As the Greeks traveled they spread the culture of winemaking throughout the Mediterranean. One of the places they planted vineyards was the port of Marsilla (now Marseilles), beginning the long history of French wine making.

What did the ancient wines taste like? It's impossible to know for sure, of course, but some things are probable. The most common wine of the ancient world was probably a sweet white wine, perhaps closest to today's German wines in taste. It was usually diluted with water, often seawater. The ancient Greeks and Romans liked to flavor their wine: Absinthe, rose petals, violets, mint, pepper — even pine resin — were favorite flavorings. Although the techniques of wine making were developed in the ancient world, the varieties of wine that we enjoy today have their roots in medieval Europe.

## Modern Origins

Wine has long been associated with religion. With the advent of Christianity, wine took on even greater symbolism as the centerpiece of the Eucharist. By the first millennium, wine was such an integral part of the social order that Charlemagne deeded vast tracts of land to the church in both France and Germany for the purpose of viticulture.

Vineyards were planted on those lands, which became such famous winemaking regions as Burgundy and Schloss Johannisberg. Tended by monks, these vineyards added greatly to both the enjoyment and the wealth of the church.

When Eleanor of Aquitaine married Henry II of England, part of her dowry included the city of Bordeaux. The importation of wine from that port created a demand in England for French wines. Those from the Bordeaux region became known in England as claret, for the clarity of the wine.

When the Spanish began to explore

the New World, they spread both Christianity and wine making to the American continents. Father Junipero Serra planted the first vines in California in 1769, at his mission of San Diego. This particular strain, the Mission grape, did not make a very good wine. Still, the Californian climate and soil was very favorable to the growth of the plant, and before long, vineyards up and down the California coast were producing grapes.

In the nineteenth century, the first vines were imported from France, and a better quality of American wine was produced. But around that time, disaster struck the wine industry.

## A Pox on Wine

The *phylloxera,* a small louse that feeds upon grapevine roots, migrated to Europe when American grapevines *(vinis lambrusca)* were imported. This insect found the European grapevines tasty and devastated the great vineyards.

When European vines were imported to California, the louse rode back in a shipment of infected vines. It began wreaking havoc on the newly planted California vineyards, just as it had in Europe.

Luckily, the indigenous American vinis lambrusca was immune to the phylloxera. Grape growers learned to graft the more delicate European varieties onto the trunks of the American plants. Today, almost all *vinis vinifera* (European grapevines) plants in the world are grafted onto vinis lambrusca trunks.

By 1911, California wines were beginning to win international competitions, but the enactment of Prohibition in 1919 was nearly as deadly to the American wine-making industry as the phylloxera louse had been. Only a few

wineries stayed in business during this period, and then only by making wine strictly for sacramental or medicinal purposes. Since the repeal of Prohibition, wine making in the United States has grown to the point where American wine makers rival their European counterparts in both volume produced and quality.

From its humble beginnings in the shadow of Mount Ararat, wine has has become the truly universal drink, produced in every continent outside of Antarctica, and forming a common bond between civilized men and women from all cultures.

# The Winemaker's Art

## The Wine-making Process

A fine wine is created by the interaction of different elements, all found naturally within grapes. There must be a certain amount of sugar, balanced with acid, for fermentation to take place. (In some wines, sugar is added to the grapes to bring up the sugar level, a practice called *chaptalization*. But this is not allowed in the finest wines.)

Grapes are harvested when their sugar/acid ratio is at its peak. The juice, called must, is pressed from the grapes and allowed to ferment.

During fermentation, yeasts, which occur naturally on the skin of the grapes, convert the sugar in the grapes into alcohol. Fermentation may stop after just a few days, or may continue for months, depending on the grapes and the type of wine desired. In general, the longer the fermentation, the less sweet the wine will be.

After the fermentation, the wine is aged — traditionally in wooden casks, but often today in stainless-steel vats — for a period of time before bottling.

This is the basic method for making wine. Different types of wine — red, white, champagne, brandy, port — vary the process according to their specific needs.

## Red Wines

All grapes produce clear juice. The coloring of red wine comes from the skin of red or black grapes. To that end — and to add greater and more complex flavor to the wine — the grape skins, seeds, and sometimes stems remain with the must while it ferments. After a period of several weeks, the wine is siphoned into a different container, thus separating it from most of the sediments. Because this process never fully rids the wine of sediments, fine red wine usually needs to be decanted before serving.

## White Wines and Rosés

White wine may be made from either white grapes or red grapes. When made from red grapes, the must is separated immediately from the skins and other sediments, to prevent the wine from picking up more than the slightest hint of color.

A rosé can be made simply by mixing white and red wine, but the best rosés are created in a process very similar to that used for white wines. The only real difference is that the must is allowed to sit with the skins for a short period, usually about a day. This imparts a pale pink tone to the juice.

## Champagnes
## and Sparkling Wines

The only true champagnes come from the Champagne region in France and are produced through the traditional *méthode champenoise*.

A base wine, called a *cuvée*, is allowed to ferment once. When that process is complete, the cuvée is bottled, stacked horizontally, and allowed to ferment again. In earlier times, when bottle making was not as precise an art as it is today, one in five bottles could be expected to explode during this period, making the method not only expensive, but dangerous as well.

As the second fermentation nears completion, the bottles are carefully turned upside down. The sediment collects in the neck of the bottle. The bottles are chilled until an ice plug, containing the sediment, is created in the neck of the bottle. The cap is removed from the bottle and the ice plug is blown out by the gases trapped behind it.

A small amount of sweet wine (called the dosage) is added to the bottle, which is then corked. A wire hood is added to help keep the cork in place.

Another less traditional method is to allow the second fermentation to take place, then remove the wine from the bottle, filter it, and rebottle it. This is called the transfer method. Another way to produce sparkling wine is to ferment the wine in large tanks. This is known as the Charmat process.

To make sure you are getting a true champagne, first make sure that it comes from the Champagne region. Second, the words "méthode champenoise" should appear on the label. Another clue is the sentence "Fermented in *this* bottle." Sparking wine produced through the transfer method carries the sentence "Fermented in *the* bottle," and those produced through the Charmat process won't mention bottles at all.

## Brandies

Brandy is actually a distilled spirit, rather than a wine. It can be created from either white wine or the residue from a pressing. The wine or residue is heated in a specially designed container until it evaporates. The vapor forms the base for the brandy. The brandy is then aged in wooden casks for several years. The casks, being porous, tend to absorb the alcohol during the process, and new brandy must be added periodically. The wood imparts a rich brown color and flavor to the brandy, which is bottled only after several years of aging.

## Ports and Sherries

Ports and sherries are fortified wines, created by the addition of brandy to a base wine in order to raise the level of alcohol. The difference between port and sherry is determined by whether the brandy is added before or after fermentation has taken place.

In the case of a port, the brandy is added before fermentation. Since this raises the alcohol level, the fermentation doesn't last long enough to convert all the sugar into alcohol, producing a very sweet, heavy wine.

In sherry, the brandy is added after fermentation to stabilize the wine. The rich brown color and nutty taste of sherry comes from a further process called maderization. Maderization may be caused either by the presence of a certain type of yeast known as Flor yeast or by a baking process (either in the sun or in an oven). The former is used traditionally in Spain, while the latter is an American innovation.

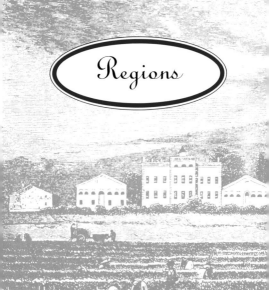

# Regions

## FRANCE

When one thinks of France, one immediately thinks of fine wine. Many of the finest vineyards are located in France, and most modern wine-making techniques were developed there. Although France produces millions of gallons of low-quality wine intended for mass consumption, its reputation for fine wines is well deserved. Its best wines are the finest in the world.

France has stringent laws to regulate the quality of the wines produced there. There are three main classifications of French wine, *Appellation d'Origine Contrôlée (AOC)*, *Vins Delimités de Qualité Supérieure (VDQS)*, and *Vins de Pays*.

---

AOC denotes the highest quality wines. This classification is limited to certain boundaries, certain grape varieties within those areas, and certain winemaking techniques. For instance, although Pinot Noir grapes are grown in both Champagne and Burgundy, red wine made from Pinot Noir in Champagne cannot have AOC status. Only white sparkling wine made in Champagne may carry that designation.

Even within those limits, there are further limits on how much wine may carry the AOC distinction. Only about fifteen percent of all French wine is awarded the *Appellation Contrôlée*. If a crop yields more wine than the law allows, the overrun must be made into vinegar or brandy. Generally speaking, the finer the label, the less that is allowed to be made. This helps keep the demand for fine French wines high by limiting the supply.

These wines may carry other distinctions as well. They may be labeled *Grand*

*Cru* (great growth), *Premier Cru* (first-quality growth), or *Deuxieme Cru* (second quality). The distinction between Grand and Premier varies from region to region. In some areas, Grand Cru is superior to Premier Cru, in others it is reversed, and sometimes wines are labeled *Grand Premier Cru*. But, in any case, by buying a French wine with the

words "Appellation Contrôlée" on the label, one is assured of buying a very fine wine.

VDQS denotes a wine of superior, but not highest, quality. A small number of French wines are awarded this status. While some of these wines are exported, most of the wine imported to the United States from France is of the highest quality.

Now that we've reviewed the different classifications of French wines, let's look at the specific regions. These are Champagne, Alsace, Chablis, Bordeaux, Burgundy, the Loire Valley, the Rhône Valley, Provence, and Languedoc. Of these, most of the finest wines come from Burgundy and Champagne.

## Burgundy
Burgundy's reputation comes mainly from the quality of its red wines. After the French Revolution, Burgundy's huge vineyards were divided into small parcels, each individually owned. Each vintner would use his own grapes to create wine, yielding a rich diversity in wines even from one vineyard. Although the modern trend is toward centralization, many wines are still made by individual wineries.

The finest region of Burgundy is Côte

d'Or, which literally translates to "hills of gold," and is also known as the "Golden Slope." The gently rolling hills of Côte d'Or produce only Pinot Noir grapes. But from this one grape, hundreds of different wines, each with individual characteristics, are created. These wines are produced in very small amounts, and are in much demand. They are the most expensive in the world.

White burgundies must not be overlooked. Some of the finest white wines available come from this region, specifically from central Burgundy, home of the great Meursaults and Montrachets.

Certainly the most popular burgundies come from the Beaujolais region. These crisp, fresh, fruity wines have been heavily promoted in the past few years, and justly so. The arrival of the light and pleasant *Beaujolais Nouveau* each November is the highlight of many American wine drinkers' year.

## Bordeaux
The Bordeaux wine region centers on the city of Bordeaux in the southwest corner

of France. It is the largest region in the world producing fine wine and is celebrated for both its reds and whites. Bordeaux accounts for about half of all the AOC wines in France.

Bordeaux, unlike Burgundy, is composed of many large estates, called châteaux. In 1855, several of these estates were designated "First Growth," denoting top-quality status. The estates of Château Lafite-Rothschild, Château Haut-Brion, Château Margaux, and Château Latour were awarded first-growth status for their red wines. Château d'Yquem was awarded first-growth status for its white wines, the only estate so honored. Since that time, the only other château added to the list is the estate Château Mouton-Rothschild, which was elevated in 1973.

The best reds from Bordeaux are produced from Cabernet Sauvignon, Merlot, Carbernet Franc, Malbec, and Petit Verdot grapes. The best whites are derived from Sauvignon Blanc and Semillon.

## Champagne
Ninety-five percent of the wine produced in Champagne is sparkling white. A small amount of red still champagne is produced, but it is without distinction.

Of the sparkling wines, eighty percent are designated AOC. Champagne is produced from two grape varieties, Chardonnay and Pinot Noir. Usually champagne wines are white, but some sparkling rosés are made.

## Alsace

One of the more unusual wine districts, Alsace is located in the northeastern part of France. Isolated by the Vosges Mountains, this area is in many ways a small bit of Germany in France. Its history reflects the cultural duality of the region. Up to the late 1600s, Alsace was a part of Germany. It became part of France after the Thirty Years War. Following the Franco-Prussian War, Alsace became part of Germany, and remained so until the end of World War I, when Alsace became French again. It has remained part of France ever since.

This history is reflected in the wines of Alsace. Alsace produces white wines almost exclusively, and mainly from grapes of German origin. The best of these are the Gewürztraminer and the Johannisberg Riesling. The Gewürztraminer wines from Alsace are better than those produced anywhere else in the world.

# GERMANY

France is composed of so many wine regions, producing such a vast and bewildering variety of wines, that one turns to Germany almost with relief for its relative simplicity. The colder German climate makes it a challenge to grow anything there, and only a few varieties of grapes are cultivated. Ninety percent of all German wines are white. But what Germany lacks in diversity and abundance, it makes up for in quality.

Because of the shortness of the growing season in Germany, grapes there must be harvested without reaching an acceptable level of sugar. This deficiency is counteracted by chaptalization, the addition of sugar in the wine-making process. This process is strictly regulated, and most of the superior growths are not allowed any added sugar.

There are two main distinctions in the quality of wine, *Tafelwein* (table wine) and *Qualitatswein*. Qualitatswein wine is divided into two subcategories, *Qualitatswein bestimmter Anbaugebiete*, or QbA (quality wine of designated regions), and *Qualitatswein mit Pradikat*, or QmP (quality wine with special qualifications).

QbA wines originate from one of the eleven regions of Germany and must be made from government-approved grape varieties. These wines are tested before they are designated. The grapes must

have achieved sufficient ripeness to result in wine that has the typical style of bouquet and flavor that is traditional to the region. Chaptalization is also permitted.

The QmP is awarded only to the very finest wines of Germany. These wines are tested each year by experts. If they do not have sufficient quality that year, they are downgraded. Unike the QbA designation, QmP wines may not be chaptalized.

All Qualitatswein must be tested by the government at a regional analysis laboratory. A certificate number is awarded to each wine. The last two digits of this number refer to the vintage year.

❧

QmP wine may also carry one of six special descriptions upon the label. These descriptions are:

*Kabinett*: Dry, white wine made from grapes at the peak of ripeness.

*Spatlese*: Relatively dry wine from grapes picked at least seven days after peak harvest. These grapes are naturally sweeter and produce a sweeter wine than Kabinett.

*Auslese*: Somewhat sweet wine made from late-harvest grapes that are specially selected.

*Beernauslese*: Literally "berry selection." Wines made from auslese grapes that are infected with *edelfäule*, a type of mold. These grapes are handpicked very late to increase their sweetness. These wines are sweet and expensive.

*Trockenbeernauslese*: Wine made from grapes infected with edelfäule and dried to a raisinlike form. These wines are very, very sweet and very, very expensive.

*Eiswein*: Literally "ice wine." These wines are made from grapes that are harvested while frozen on the vine.

## ITALY

Although Italy is a world leader in both production and consumption of wine, much of its exported wine is ordinary and without distinction, charm, or finesse.

Part of the problem may be that so much of the crop is consumed locally. Without the pressure of competition, there is little need for innovation and improvement. Wine making in Italy predates the Roman Empire and has changed little from then to today.

In 1963, the Italian government enacted a body of laws called *Demoninazione di Origine Controllata* (DOC).

To qualify, a particular region must be capable of producing wines of a certain merit, employing particular wine-making techniques. The DOC is the equivalent to, but not the equal of, the French AOC designation.

Perhaps the most popular Italian wine

is the Tuscan Chianti. "Popular" is the key word here, although there are many excellent Chiantis available. Those Chiantis labeled *Riserva* are aged in oak casks and take on a subtle orange flavor that is well worth trying.

Other fine wines from Italy include Brunello di Montalcino and Vino Nobile di Montepulciano, both made from Brunello grapes. They resemble full-bodied Rhône wines.

Two excellent red Italian table wines come from Valpolicella and Bardolino. Valpolicellas are light and fruity; Bardolinos, equally pleasant, are meant to be drunk when fresh and slightly chilled.

## SPAIN

Some of the finest wines from Spain come from the Rioja district. This region was settled by French wine makers fleeing the phylloxera plague in France in the late nineteenth century. Landing in the Rioja district, they began making wines in the French style, aging the wine in large wooden casks. These wines are becoming popular now in the United States because of their good quality and low price. Spain is also known for its sherries and inexpensive sparkling wines, which are made in the traditional méthode champenoise.

## PORTUGAL

Portugal is best known for port and inexpensive rosés, but some other wines are quite distinctive. The popular *vinho verdes* (green wine) have a slight effervescence due to secondary fermentation in the bottle.

# UNITED STATES
## California

The time was, when one thought of American wines one immediately thought of California jug wines. No longer. While it is true that much wine in California is mass-produced, the finest California wines hold their own with the finest wines in the world.

The wine regions of California can be divided into four main areas — north coast, south coast, central coast, and central valley. The central valley is the home of the major wine producers, known for quantity rather than quality. The largest of these is Gallo, which has a bottling capacity of three million bottles a day.

The north coast, north of San Francisco, has the best reputation for fine wine. Napa Valley produces wines in the

French tradition, while Sonoma County wines show an Italian influence. Although almost all types of grapes are grown in California, the most popular grape from that state in the past few years has been the Zinfandel, made into a mildly sweet blush wine. Perhaps the most popular California reds are made from Cabernet Sauvignon grapes; the most popular whites are Chardonnays.

## The Northwest

The states of the Pacific Northwest — Oregon and Washington — have started producing quality wines in the last two decades. Unlike California, where wine making is a huge and established industry, wine making in the Northwest is more like a cottage industry, with many small vineyards producing small amounts of quality wines. The Pinot Noir wines are particularly fine; some Oregon Pinot Noirs have won international awards.

## SOUTH AMERICA

Chile is well suited to producing Bordeaux varieties. Chilean Riesling emerges fresh and dry, austere, and similar in style to German Steinwein. Chilean reds in the French style, headed by Merlot and Cabernet Sauvignon, have been singled out internationally.

Argentina is the fourth-largest wine-producing country in the world. It is also home to heavy wine consumers, with a per capita consumption of twenty-two gallons a year. Little Argentine wine is exported; that which is is often coarse and volatile.

## AUSTRALIA

Australians make some of the best sherry outside of Europe. "Down Under" is becoming known for some other wines as well.

Years ago, Australian wine makers went after the inexpensive, jug-wine market dominated by the giant California vineyards. They have recently tended to turn inward, experimenting with small, quality vineyards and developing fine wines. Australian table wines — particularly reds — are beginning to rival the best from France and California.

Barossa Valley, one of the better wine-producing regions, shows a heavy German influence in its culture and wines. The Cabernets from Coonawarra are outstanding, while the Hunter River Valley excels in wines made with Shiraz and Semillon grapes.

Grapes

❦

# A Guide
## to the Common Varieties of
## Wine-Producing Grapes

*Cabernet Franc*: A red vinifera grape. It produces wines that are rounder and softer than the Cabernet Sauvignon, to which it is related.

*Cabernet Sauvignon*: A red vinifera grape. The best of the Cabernet family. This grape is the predominant ingredient in the best red Bordeaux wines. It is at its best when used at close to 100 percent, but it can be blended with other grapes. The grapes are spicy, herbaceous, and tannic. Wines made from very ripe grapes are often minty and cedary, with a black currant or cassis character.

*Carignan*: The most widely planted grape in France, this yields very ordinary, coarse wine. Also planted in California, where it is blended into jug wines.

*Chardonnay*: A white grape of exceptional quality. This is the only grape permitted by French law to be used in Chablis wines. It is also grown in Champagne, where it is used to make Blanc de Blanc. It is planted widely in California, where it makes the best Californian white wines.

*Chenin Blanc*: A white grape planted in the Loire Valley, where it is used for both still and sparkling wines. It is the only grape permitted in Anjou white wines. Its aroma is reminiscent of fresh peaches. Popular in California, Australia, South Africa, and South American countries.

*Gamay*: A red grape planted in France and California, it produces fresh and delightful young red wines in Beaujolais, but is quite ordinary otherwise.

*Gewürztraminer*: A clone of the *Traminer* grape with a distinctive spicy and floral aroma. It is particularly sensitive to its soil, location, and growing techniques. The best Gewürztraminer wines come from the Alsace region in France, although the grape is also grown widely in Germany.

*Grenache*: A red grape of Spanish origin. In Spain it is known as the Garnacha and is blended to produce Rioja. In the Rhône Valley it is used to produce Tavel, a rosé, which at its best is a full-bodied, assertive wine. In California, the grape is blended to produce rosé and some ports.

*Johannisberg Riesling*: A white grape, often called Riesling, or White Riesling in California. It is particularly sensitive to soil and vineyard location. Riesling grapes grown even on the same hillside can produce completely different wines. Its best wines have depth and intensity, with delicate aromas evoking apricots or fresh peaches. But if it is unripe, the wine can be very dry and austere. In Germany, the former style is preferred; in Alsace, the latter is produced.

*Merlot*: A red grape from France but grown in many wine regions. Sometimes it is used as a mellowing agent in blends with Cabernet Sauvignon, but it can be

made into a varietal wine. The greatest of
these wines come from Pomerol and St.
Emilion.

*Müller-Thurgau*: A white grape, said to
be a cross between the Sylvaner and the
Johannisberg Riesling. It has become the
most cultivated vine in Germany. Rip-
ening earlier than the Riesling, it produces a soft, flowery wine.

*Muscat*: A family of white grapes, in-
cluding Muscat Blanc, Moscato, and
Muscadelle. This family can produce
wines of great variety, from subtle to
overpowering, from dry to very sweet. In
Italy, these grapes are used to make Asti
Spumante. In Alsace, they produce a dry

white. Their aroma is pungent and sometimes spicy.

*Palomino*: A white grape sometimes called Golden Chasselas. Developed around Jerez de la Frontera, Spain, this grape is used primarily for sherry, both in Spain and California.

*Pinot Blanc*: A white grape, related to the Pinot Noir. It is called Weissburgunder in Germany and Pinot Bianco or sometimes Pinot a'Alba in Italy, where it produces good-quality sparkling wines. It is used in California for champagne cuvées.

*Pinot Gris*: A white grape, related to the Pinot Noir. It is called Tokay in Alsace, Tocai in Italy and Yugoslavia, and Rilander in Germany. Although it is related to the stellar Pinot Noir, the white wines produced from this grape are often without distinction.

*Pinot Noir:* A black grape, known as Spätburgunder in Germany. It can produce both red and white wines. In France it is the principal ingredient in Côte d'Or wines, the best and most expensive reds in the world. It is used as the base for all true champagnes (with the exception of

Blanc de Blanc, which is made with Chardonnay). Is has been planted in California without much success, but has achieved international distinction in Oregon wines.

*Riesling*: See Johannisberg Riesling.

*Sauvignon Blanc*: A white grape, grown in France and California. In Bordeaux, this grape is used in the dry white wine of Graves and blended with Semillon to produce great Sauternes. In California, wines made with this grape are usually called Fumé Blanc.

*Semillon*: A white grape, known also as the Riesling in Australia. In its normal state, this grape yields dry white wines.

In its overripe state it can take on a noble rot, called *pourriture noble*. This state is necessary to produce classic Sauterne dessert wines.

*Sylvaner*: A white grape widely cultivated in Germany. It is easier to grow than the Johannisberg Riesling, but the wines produced are without distinction.

*Syrah*: A red grape integral to the finer Rhône Valley wines. The Syrah is used in South Africa's finest red wines. In Australia it is known as the Shiraz or Hermitage grape.

*Traminer*: Favored in the Rhine, Alsace, and the Italian Tyrol, this grape has a spicy aroma. It was once widely planted, but is being supplanted by the Gewürztraminer, which produces a more distinctive wine.

*White Riesling*: See Johannisberg Riesling.

*Zinfandel*: A variety of red grape, it is the most widely planted of all red-wine grapes in California, but is not grown commercially anywhere else. Its best wines are heady and rich in flavor, evocative of blackberries with a hint of spiciness.

# Wine and Food

## Selecting A Wine

There is one rule to follow when choosing a wine: Select one that you enjoy. Beyond that, a few general guidelines might be of assistance when making your selection.

*For lunch and light meals,* choose a lighter, dry wine, either a white or a young red.

*When serving a variety of wines at a meal,* white wines are usually served before reds. This is because the whites tend to be crisper and simpler, whetting the appetite. The red wines are usually heavier and more complex and benefit from the contemplation that occurs nearer the end of a meal or after it.

*Young wines usually are served before old wines.* This is because the simpler flavors of the young wines can be overwhelmed by the mellowness and rich, round taste of a more mature wine.

*Fish* usually is accompanied well by a dry, white wine. A rich shellfish, lobster, or crab complemented with a dry Chablis is a particularly fine contrast.

While white wines usually are chosen to *contrast* with food, reds are chosen to *complement* the main course. An herby red will bring out the spices in a roast and vice versa.

It is very difficult to match any wine with some foods. But it is possible to point out certain combinations that should be avoided:

- *oily fish and red wine*
- *asparagus and any wine*
- *salads with a vinegar-based dressing and any wine*
- *citrus fruits and wine*
- *highly spiced foods, such as oriental or Indian food, and delicate wines*

*And be sure to avoid combining wine and chocolate — two great tastes that do **not** taste great together!*

### Storing Wine

Wine should be stored in a cool, dry place, with an optimum temperature of 54°F. Wine bottles should always be stored on their sides, in order to prevent corks from drying and allowing air to enter the bottle and spoil the wine.

An unfinished bottle of opened wine, whether red or white, should be stored in the refrigerator in order to preserve freshness.

If by some chance you should open and not finish a bottle of champagne, you can restore its fizz the next day by dropping a raisin in the bottle. The sugar in the raisin rejuvenates the wine without flavoring it.

## Serving Wine
Serving a fine wine takes planning. After selecting the wine for a meal, care and time must be taken to make sure the wine is presented at its best.

Opening the bottle requires some care, since many things can go wrong.

The cork may break and stick in the neck, or worse, break apart and fall into the wine. The worst of all is when the cork proves so stubborn that the bottle must be placed between the legs and the corkscrew pulled on until one is red in the face. To avoid this, take care in choosing a corkscrew. There are several kinds. The best ones have long, wide-bored worms that grip the cork securely, and some kind of leverage system to aid in pulling the cork.

## Popping the Bubbly

Opening a champagne bottle provides an entirely different set of challenges, since the main problem is not getting the cork out, but preventing it from popping out and breaking something. The gases in a champagne bottle are so strong that the cork must be held in place with a wire cage.

First, wrap the bottle in a towel or linen napkin. The chances that the bottle will explode are minimal, but it only needs to happen once. Wrapping the bottle helps protect the person opening the bottle, and any other people who are around. Point the bottle away from yourself and anybody else. Do not point the bottle toward windows, fine china, or anything breakable.

Holding the bottle near the bottom, or butt, gently remove the wire hood from the cork. Take hold of the cork, and gently twist the bottle and pull it away from the cork. The bottle and cork should separate with a gentle pop and a whiff of smoke. The cork should not shoot out of the bottle, propelled by a foaming geyser. The effect may be spectacular, but it is a waste of good wine.

## To Decant

Fine red wines often need to be decanted to separate the wine from the sediments at the bottom of the bottle. This must be planned in advance, since the bottle should be placed upright and allowed to sit for several hours before decanting.

The basic tools for decanting are a decanter, a bottle opener, and a candle (or better yet, a strong flashlight). Place the light next to the decanter so that it will shine through the neck of the bottle as you pour. Then open the bottle and pour it slowly into the decanter.

Keep your eye on the neck of the bottle. As the level in the bottle goes down, a dark line (the sediment) will appear. This is your cue to stop. A decanted wine should be as clear as possible. It is nice, even when a wine is decanted, to have the bottle present at the table, so that those enjoying the wine can know the vintage.

## To Breathe or Not to Breathe

Once the wine is decanted, should it be exposed to the air and allowed to "breathe" or not? Authorities differ on this point. The more exposed to the air, the more the flavors of the wine will dissipate. On the other hand, some wines definitely need a little mellowing. The safest course is to avoid letting the wine breathe before it is served. That way, you can be sure that the wine will be as flavorful as possible. If it does need to breathe, let it breathe in the glasses. Fine wine should be savored, not hurried. If it takes a long time to drink the bottle, all the better.

Temperature is another important factor to consider when drinking wine. Red wine is usually served at room temperature, between sixty-five and seventy degrees Fahrenheit. White wines and rosés are usually chilled to about 45°F. This can be done either in a refrigerator or an ice bucket. Do not chill any wine in a freezer. Forgotten bottles may explode.

## Ordering Wine in a Restaurant

Ordering wine in a restaurant can be a traumatic experience. Before investing in an expensive bottle, try a glass of the house white wine prior to the meal. It will be indicative of the general quality of the wines offered. If it is below your standard, you may be able to bring your own wine to the restaurant. Inquire, as some restaurants do not permit this.

Any decent wine list should provide complete information about the wines offered. This includes the village, vintage, vintner, and merchant. Try to have a second choice, in case the first bottle turns out not to be what you wanted.

If you are very familiar with the restaurant and its wine list, you may want to call ahead so that the restaurant can have time to decant the wine.

# Glassware

There are no hard and fast rules about which glass to use with which variety of wine, but a few general guidelines should be kept in mind. Choose a glass with a large enough bowl to get a good serving without filling it to the brim. The bowl should taper slightly toward the top, to help contain the aromas of the wine. In general, avoid cut glass or colored glass. These interfere with the color of the wine.

And remember the old saying: When pouring wine, leave room for the nose! A glass filled to the brim should be reserved for beer and other rude beverages.

The following are traditional glass

shapes associated with the different types of wine.

## Glassware

White Wine

Red Bordeaux

White Burgundy

Red Burgundy

# A Wine Drinker's Glossary

*Here is a smattering of the many and varied ways to describe wine.*

---

*Acetic*: Having an excessively sharp and vinegary taste.

*Astringent*: Refers to a mouth-puckering sensation, caused by the tannin in red wine. Usually occurs with young wines, which mellow as they age.

*Austere*: Used to refer to wines that are undeveloped, with little or no nuance in flavor.

*Balanced*: Refers to the combination of the components of wine—fruit, acid, tannin, alcohol, etc. Wines that have these components in a very pleasing combination are called well balanced. Those in which one predominates are called unbalanced.

*Clean*: Having an absence of foreign and unpleasant odors.

*Complex*: Containing many facets of taste and smell in a pleasing combination.

*Dry*: Not sweet.

*Dumb*: Describes a wine that is immature, but that carries the potential of quality.

*Earthy*: A pleasant characteristic, evoking the smell of freshly turned soil.

*Fat*: Having a full body, with the alcohol and/or glycerols overshadowing the acidity of the wine.

*Finesse*: An abstract quality that separates a great wine from a merely good wine.

*Firm*: Refers to a good balance between alcohol and acid in wine. The opposite of flabby.

*Flabby*: Lacking sufficient acid to properly balance the alcohol, extract, or sweetness.

*Flat*: Lacking acidity. A wine that is dull and lifeless.

*Flowery*: Having a fragrant, flower-like smell.

*Fresh*: Having a lively and youthful quality to the nose or palate.

*Fruity*: Describes a rich, fleshy quality coming from ripe grapes, but not necessarily a grapelike smell.

*Full-bodied*: Refers to a wine that has a mouth-filling feel. A wine with a high alcohol and extract content.

*Hollow*: Having a strong first taste and after-taste, but no middle taste.

*Maderized*: Refers to a wine with a heavy, flat, "brown" smell, which is usually overmature.

*Nutty*: Having a crisp, rounded flavor and the smell of cobnuts.

*Peardrops*: An undesirable characteristic, indicating a poorly made white wine. Gives off the smell of spirit gum.

*Peppery*: Describes a raw quality in young wines with high alcohol content, which causes a reaction on the nose not unlike pepper.

*Prickly*: Having a sharp, raw, acidic quality, either to the nose or palate.

*Robust*: Pleasing, coarse, and full-bodied.

*Silky*: Having a soft, but firm, texture.

*Simple*: Describes a wine that is not complex, but straightforward and without nuance. A pleasing quality.

*Smoky:* Evoking the smell of burnt wood.

*Spicy:* Having a spicelike smell, particularly noticeable in grapes of the Gewürtztraminer varieties.

*Spritzig:* Refers to wine with a slight effervescence in the mouth.

*Supple:* Having a pleasing balance of texture, vigor, and harmony in a young wine. An indication that the mature wine will be delicate and complex.

*Thin:* Lacking body; watery, a serious fault.

*Varietal:* A wine that is made mainly from one grape variety, having the distinctive aroma and taste of that variety.

*Velvety:* Silky, smooth, and opulent in texture.

*Vinous*: Having a pleasant, general wine taste, without a definite varietal quality.

*Woody*: Describes the undesirable aroma or flavor of a wine that was kept too long in the cask and has picked up the characteristics of the wood.

*Yeasty*: Refers to the smell or taste of yeast in wine. Usually undesirable, but may dissipate as the wine ages.

The text of this book
was set in Bernhard Modern
by Trufont Typographers
Hicksville, New York

Designed by:
Tilman Reitzle and Michael Hortens